HISTORICAL COMICS™

EPIC BATTLES OF THE CIVIL WAR

VOLUME 1: FIRST BULL RUN

Writers:
WILLIAM MESSNER-LOEBS
RICHARD ROCKWELL

Penciler:
RICHARD ROCKWELL

Inker:
FRED FREDERICKS

Colorist:
MARIE SEVERIN

Letterers:
JOHN COSTANZA
MICHAEL HIGGINS

Book Design:
JOE KAUFMAN
MEL SANCHEZ & VITO INCORVAIA

Assistant Editor:
RICHARD ASHFORD

Editor:
NELSON YOMTOV

Executive Editor:
CARL POTTS

Editor in Chief:
BOB HARRAS

Series Contributors:
JOHN FORD
Introductions and epilogues

GEORGE WOODBRIDGE
Consultant

Cover Artist:
NICK CHOLES
*Pen & Ink Reproduction of
a painting by Earl Norem*

Cover Colorist:
MIKE THOMAS

Special Thanks to:
JOHN LEWANDOWSKI

*Photographs of Generals P.G.T. Beauregard, Irwin McDowell and Thomas "Stonewell" Jackson
courtesy of The Civil War Library and Museum, Philadelphia, PA.*

This book was produced in cooperation with Marvel Entertainment Group, Inc.

Separations by American Color, Buffalo, NY.

P9-CDP-060

INTRODUCTION

On December 20, 1860, a special edition of the Charleston, South Carolina newspaper the *Mercury* announced in huge letters that THE UNION IS DISSOLVED! South Carolina had seceded, declared itself no longer a part of the United States of America. Within a month, six more states (Mississippi, Florida, Alabama, Georgia, Louisiana, and Texas) seceded as well, and on February 4, 1861 representatives met at Montgomery, Alabama to write a constitution and form a government—the Confederate States of America.

The Confederacy insisted that the U.S.A. had always been a voluntary organization of independent states, any of whom had the right to leave if it wished. The key issue in the winter of 1860 was slavery. For forty years, a series of political compromises had tried to balance the desire of slaveholders to keep their "peculiar [that is, special] institution" with that of others, mostly in the North, to limit or end it. But the compromises had only put off a solution to the problem. When Abraham Lincoln, known to be against slavery, was elected President in 1860, the slave states decided not to wait any longer for action.

What was left of the United States still had military bases in the Confederacy. The land forts could not be supplied or reinforced, and passed to Confederate control. But one costal stronghold, Fort Sumter, stood on an island in the entrance to Charleston harbor, the most important seaport in the Confederacy.

In April, President Lincoln decided to force a showdown: he announced that Sumter would be resupplied by sea. The Confederate President, Jefferson Davis, ordered his commanding officer in Charleston, Pierre G. T. Beauregard, to demand Sumter surrender. The negotiations failed, and on April 12, 1861 cannons began bombarding the fort. Two days later, it surrendered.

Both Union and Confederacy were now committed to a war to either end or support secession. Indeed, many seemed to have expected fighting from the first. Lt. General Winfield Scott, General in Chief of the Army, prepared a master plan to blockade Southern ports and slowly starve the Confederacy, but most thought the plan too slow. The nation was in danger; it must be fought for, the issue must be settle *now*. The *New York Tribune* made the slogan "Forward to Richmond!," the Confederate capital, a regular part of its front page.

Armies were hastily assembled on both sides. Union volunteers signed up for ninety days' service — an indication of how long the war was expected to last.

By July, General Irvin McDowell commanded an army of 35,000 men—twice the size of the pre-war Regular Army — camped near Washington, DC. A Confederate army of 20,000 under General Beauregard was twenty-five miles away, in the railroad center of Manassas, Virginia, by a creek called Bull Run. Urged to attack the Rebels, McDowell pointed out that his men were barely trained, and some of his officers hardly more so; General McDowell had until recently been a major, and many of his colonels had been lieutenants in the pre-war army. President Lincoln told him, "You are green, it is true, but they are green also; you are all green alike." On July 16, the army began to move.

The other side was not idle. Another 12,000 troops under General Joseph Johnston were about to be moved by train to reinforce Beauregard.

Union and Confederate were both determined that their cause was right enough to fight for and, on the morning of July 21, most of them also thought things would be decided in a few more hours.

"I RECOGNIZED THEM. THEY WERE 'GAY' LADIES. RESIDENTS OF MRS. JUPITER'S BOARDING HOUSE. AMONG THEM WAS ANNIE CROOKSTER."

BEST BE OFF, MATTY.

OH, LOOK! THERE'S LAWTON.

BET THE REBS ARE SORRY THEY STARTED THIS WAR.

YEP. WE'LL SCATTER 'EM LIKE RABBITS. HOPE THEY STAY AROUND LONG ENOUGH TO MAKE A REAL FIGHT OF IT.

"MATTY BUDD WASN'T THE FIRST TO SAY SO. THE NORTH WAS FULL OF SUCH SENTIMENT."

"HORACE GREELEY, EDITOR OF THE NEW YORK TRIBUNE, ALWAYS SAID WHAT WAS ON HIS MIND..."

New-York Daily Tribune

SUNDAY, JUNE 30, 1861.

THE NATION'S WAR-CRY.

Forward to Richmond! Forward to Richmon *The Rebel Congress must not be allowed to me there on the 20th of July!* BY THAT DATE TH PLACE MUST BE HELD BY THE NATIONAL ARMY

IT IS TIME, SIR! IT IS PAST TIME FOR US TO STRIKE AND WIPE THE EVIL OF SLAVERY FROM THE FACE OF THIS WIDE EARTH!

AS A LEADING ANTI-SLAVERY PROPONENT, DO YOU BELIEVE THAT THE BLACK MAN SHOULD BE PERMITTED TO ENLIST IN THIS WAR?

I BELIEVE THAT ABOLITION OF SLAVERY IS A MORAL CRUSADE. EVERY NORTHERN BLACK IS AN ABOLITION-IST. IF THE WAR PERSISTS, WE WILL NEED THE HELP OF EVERY ABLE-BODIED MAN.

"I LEFT GREELEY AND JOURNEYED TO WASHINGTON, WHERE I SPOKE WITH FREDERICK DOUGLASS, LEADER OF THE BLACK ABOLITIONISTS AND EDITOR OF THE NORTH STAR..."

THE WICKEDNESS OF SLAVERY IS TEARING THE UNION APART. I HAVE JUST WRITTEN TO MR. LINCOLN NOW THAT THE WAR HAS BEGUN. I SUGGESTED I COULD ORGANIZE SLAVE REVOLTS THROUGHOUT THE SOUTH.

THE UNION IS FIGHTING THE REBELS WITH ONLY ONE HAND WHEN THEY REFUSE TO RECEIVE THE VERY CLASS OF MEN WHICH HAVE A DEEPER INTEREST IN THE DEFEAT AND HUMILIATION OF THE REBELS THAN ALL OTHERS.

MY PEOPLE COULD HELP DESTROY THAT EVIL AND SHAMEFUL SYSTEM. BUT MR. LINCOLN FEARS THAT SLAVE REVOLTS AND BLACK SOLDIERS WOULD NOT HELP TO PRESERVE THE UNION.

" SLAVE REVOLTS, BLACK SOLDIERS, PRESERVING THE UNION... THESE ARE LINCOLN'S DILEMMAS..."

"THE PASSION TO STRIKE A BLOW AT THE REBELS WAS REACHING A FEVERED PITCH WITHIN THE UNION. EARLIER, WHEN SECESSION WAS SIMPLY A LEGAL ARGUMENT, I HAD TRAVELED TO RICHMOND TO THE OFFICES OF JEFFERSON DAVIS, PRESIDENT OF THE CONFEDERACY..."

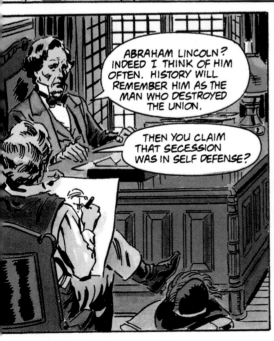

ABRAHAM LINCOLN? INDEED I THINK OF HIM OFTEN. HISTORY WILL REMEMBER HIM AS THE MAN WHO DESTROYED THE UNION.

THEN YOU CLAIM THAT SECESSION WAS IN SELF DEFENSE?

WE HAD TO. TO SAVE THE CONSTITUTION. EVERY PRESIDENT OF THIS LAND HAS RESPECTED STATES' RIGHTS -- ALL BUT LINCOLN. I FEAR HE WILL SOON DECLARE SLAVERY ILLEGAL. THIS COUNTRY WAS NOT BUILT BELIEVING THAT THE FEDERAL GOVERNMENT HAD THE RIGHT TO SEIZE PROPERTY, SUCH AS SLAVES.

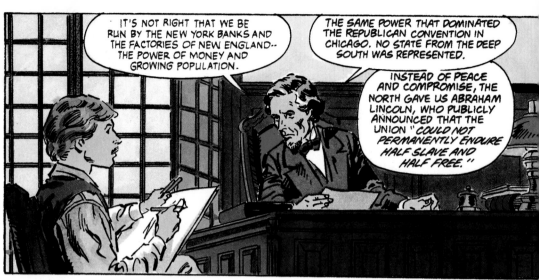

IT'S NOT RIGHT THAT WE BE RUN BY THE NEW YORK BANKS AND THE FACTORIES OF NEW ENGLAND-- THE POWER OF MONEY AND GROWING POPULATION.

THE SAME POWER THAT DOMINATED THE REPUBLICAN CONVENTION IN CHICAGO. NO STATE FROM THE DEEP SOUTH WAS REPRESENTED.

INSTEAD OF PEACE AND COMPROMISE, THE NORTH GAVE US ABRAHAM LINCOLN, WHO PUBLICLY ANNOUNCED THAT THE UNION *"COULD NOT PERMANENTLY ENDURE HALF SLAVE AND HALF FREE."*

DO YOU BELIEVE THAT LINCOLN IS MERELY A PUPPET OF ABOLITIONISTS AND MUNITIONS MAKERS?

THEY *PUT* HIM IN OFFICE. LET ME TELL YOU THIS...

IN A SPEECH IN 1838, LINCOLN PRAISED THE FOUNDING FATHERS, BUT I THINK FOR THE WRONG REASONS. WHILE HE ADMIRED THE NEW PATHS THEY CUT, HE WAS HUNGRY FOR THE GLORY THEY RECEIVED. HE SAID THAT THERE WILL BE NEW LEADERS, AND I SUSPECT HE WAS TALKING ABOUT HIMSELF, WHO WILL FIND NEW PATHS TO CUT AND NEW GLORY TO SEEK. HE SAID THEY WILL THIRST AND BURN FOR DISTINCTION, AND THEY WILL HAVE IT... "WHETHER AT THE EXPENSE OF EMANCIPATING SLAVES OR ENSLAVING FREE MEN."

THE REPUBLICANS HAVE ELECTED THIS MAN WHO SEEKS HIS OWN GLORY DESPITE THE *CERTAIN RUIN* HE'LL LEAVE BEHIND HIM. TELL *THAT* TO YOUR READERS, MR. DANIELS.

"AS I LEFT THE OFFICE OF PRESIDENT JEFFERSON DAVIS, I KNEW THERE WOULD BE NO COMPROMISE-- ONLY WAR WOULD RESOLVE THIS IMPASSE."

"THE SOUTH BEGAN THE WAR BY FIRING ON *FORT SUMTER* IN THE HARBOR AT *CHARLESTON, SOUTH CAROLINA.* I WENT STRAIGHT AWAY TO PRESIDENT LINCOLN'S WHITE HOUSE OFFICE. I SOUGHT AN ANSWER-- WOULD HE BE THE INSTRUMENT OF THE UNION'S DESTRUCTION OR THE LEADER OF ITS SALVATION?"

I'M SORRY, MR. DANIELS, THE PRESIDENT IS EXTREMELY BUSY.

I'LL WAIT, THANK YOU.

"I WENT OVER MY NOTES FROM RICHMOND AND THE CARTOON I FOUND IN A NEWSPAPER THERE..."

HMM. THE BEARDED MONKEY FROM KENTUCKY...

NOT A BAD LIKENESS. BUT THE WHISKERS HIDE MY CHIN-- I'D LOOK MORE LIKE A MONKEY WITHOUT THEM!

MR. PRESIDENT, SIR, I...

FORGIVE MY EAVES-DROPPING, BUT I LIKE TO KNOW WHAT A MAN'S THINKING BEFORE HE EXAMINES ME.

SIR, JEFFERSON DAVIS ASSERTS YOU ARE DESTROYING THE UNION.

THE CONFEDERATES ARE THE AGGRESSORS. CALL IT SECESSION OR REBELLION. IT IS, IN FACT, TREASON. I HAVE GIVEN MY OATH TO PRESERVE, PROTECT AND DEFEND THE UNION!

ARE YOU PREPARED TO RESPOND WITH FORCE TO THE CAPTURE OF FT. SUMTER?

I HAVE CALLED FOR 75,000 MEN FOR A THREE MONTH ENLISTMENT. MANY AMERICANS URGE A QUICK RESPONSE...

...BUT OUR ARMY IS GREEN. THEY NEED TIME TO LEARN HOW TO BE SOLDIERS. I SUPPOSE I STILL HOPE THAT CIVIL WAR CAN BE AVOIDED SO THEY WON'T HAVE TO FIGHT. BUT I HAVE MY DOUBTS. I HOPE FOR PEACE BUT PREPARE FOR WAR.

"I READ TO HIM THE PART OF HIS 1838 SPEECH THAT DAVIS QUOTED..."

HE SAYS YOU WANT GLORY FOR YOURSELF.

WHAT OF JEFFERSON DAVIS? PERHAPS HE HAS HIS OWN SHARE OF AMBITION.

AND SLAVERY, SIR?

WE MUST ALLOW TIME F ANTI-SLAVERY SENTIMEN TO GROW. THE UNION IS N READY TO FIGHT A WAR 1 ABOLISH SLAVERY.

JULY 18. THE UNION ARMY CAMPS AT CENTREVILLE, NEAR BULL RUN.

"FOR TWO DAYS GUNS, WAGONS AND MEN HAVE FILED INTO THE SITE. MY FELLOW TIMES CORRESPONDENT, WILLIAM HOWARD RUSSELL, EXPRESSED HIS DOUBTS ABOUT THE READINESS OF THE UNION ARMY.

REMARKABLE! A MONTH AGO THEY WE RIBBON CLERKS. NOW WITH UNIFORMS, GUNS AND TRAIN ING THEY ARE STILL RIBBO CLERKS!

"BUT HE WASN'T THE ONLY ONE TO SLIP THROUGH THE FEDERAL LINES THAT NIGHT. MY LOVELY ACQUAINTANCE WHO WISHED ME A PLEASANT STAY IN THE COUNTRY FOUND HER WAY TO GENERAL BEAUREGARD'S HEADQUARTERS AT MANASSAS JUNCTION..."

WE WERE AFRAID YOU WOULDN'T GET THROUGH THE UNION LINES.

THEY THOUGHT I WAS INNOCENT ENOUGH.

GENTLEMEN-- OUR FRIEND FROM WASHINGTON.

NOW LET US SEE THE INFORMATION YOU HAVE GATHERED.

IT WOULD SEEM THAT SCOTT AND McDOWELL ARE LIMITING THEIR NUMBERS FOR THIS BATTLE.

THEY ARE NOT EXPECTING OUR RESERVES.

NOBLE FRANKS, SIR. I CAME TO FIGHT.

GOOD, LA... FOLLOW M...

"AND A NEW RECRUIT ADDED ONE MORE TO BEAUREGARD'S RANKS."

IN ACCORDANCE WITH GENERAL McDOWELL'S PLAN, THE UNION ARTILLERY FIRES THREE SHOTS FROM THE PARROTT GUN, A RIFLED 30 POUNDER IN FRONT OF THE STONE BRIDGE. THERE IS NO REPLY FROM THE CONFEDERATES.

"WE NEWS REPORTERS REALIZED THIS WOULD MOST LIKELY BE THE DAY OF BATTLE."

IT REQUIRES NINETEEN HORSES TO PULL THE PARROTT, LAWTON.

AND IT WILL PROBABLY KILL MORE THAN 19 MEN TODAY.

"THE MASS MOVEMENT OF U[...] SOLDIERS UNDER THE COVER O[...] DARKNESS TOOK MUCH LONG[...] THAN McDOWELL HAD ANTICIP[...] BY DAWN, THE FIRST UNITS W[...] EXPECTED TO ATTACK THE CON[...] ERATE LEFT, BUT THEY WERE [...] ON THE TRAIL -- HOT, DUST-COVERED AND ALREADY TIRE[...]

WHAT THEY DIDN'T KNOW WAS THAT THE CONFEDERATE FORCES WERE WAITING FOR THEM.

I DON'T LIKE THIS STANDING AROUND. LET'S GET ON WITH IT AND FIGHT.

THE FORCES OF BEE, EVANS AND COLONEL BARTOW MERGE WITH THOSE OF JACKSON. NEARBY, CONCEALED IN PINE THICKETS, LAY THE CAVALRY OF J.E.B. STUART, CONFEDERATE COLONEL.

3 P.M. ON STONEWALL JACKSON'S COMMAND, J.E.B. STUART'S CAVALRY CHARGES DOWN ON THE NEW YORK MILITIA, KNOWN AS ZOUAVES, WHO ARE PROTECTING UNION BATTERIES OF ARTILLERY.

AS THE ZOUAVES RETREAT FROM COVERING THE ARTILLERY'S POSITION, AN OFFICER SEES A SECOND THREAT APPROACH ON HIS RIGHT.

MAJOR BARRY! TO YOUR RIGHT! TURN YOUR GUNS!

THEY'RE OURS, CAPTAIN GRIFFIN! I CAN SEE THE BLUE THEY WEAR!

THEY WILL SUPPORT US!

IT WAS NOT UNION BLUE. IT WAS VIRGINIA'S MILITIA BLUE, UNDER THE COMMAND OF STONEWALL JACKSON. MAJOR BARRY'S ERROR BECAME OBVIOUS WHEN GUNFIRE FROM 60 YARDS AWAY HIT 54 UNION MEN AND 104 HORSES.

As *IF IN ONE VOICE, A SOUND ARISES FROM EACH REBEL THROAT... A PIERCING, HOWLING SOUND THAT IS THE RELEASE OF ANGER, FRUSTRATION AND FEAR. THE BATTLE WILL BE WON OR LOST ON THIS CHARGE...*

"JEM TUTTLE AND NOBLE FRANKS WOULD FINALLY JOIN THE BATTLE."

HERE'S OUR CHANCE. FIX IT, NOBLE!

JEM, I HAVE NO BAYONET!

NO DIFFERENCE. LET'S JOIN THE LINE.

"RUSSELL AND I MOVED CLOSER TO THE BATTLE LINES."

EACH TIME I GET A SKETCH STARTED, YOU DECIDE TO MOVE, RUSSELL.

LAWTON, LISTEN! THAT SOUND-- IT'S THE REBELS! THEY'RE YELLING SOMETHING.

EPILOGUE

Once the rout began among the Federal troops at Bull Run, they began to flee, and did not stop until they reached the Potomac River, more than twenty miles away. The Washington civilians who had ridden out with their picnic baskets to watch the show helped clog the roads and carry the panic.

Some people, both at the time and later, have argued that if the Confederate soldiers had followed their beaten enemy, they might have gone to the gates of Washington and forced a settlement on the spot. Confederate President Jefferson Davis had traveled to the battlefield, and he urged his generals to press on. A Confederate army of the later war, trained and experienced, might have done so. But these were new soldiers, with new leaders. The Rebels were, as one of their generals said, almost as disorganized by their victory as the Union by defeat. They were not only tired, but almost out of ammunition and food — some of them did not eat for a full day after the battle.

Also, McDowell had fresh reserves at Centreville, and the Potomac River was well-fortified against such an attack. (One of the many odd facts about the war is that the two national capitals, Washington and Richmond, were only a hundred miles apart. Despite various proposed attacks and raids, neither would be directly attacked until Richmond was finally evacuated a few days before the end of the war.)

Lessons in war are learned only with difficulty and great expense. It is easier for us, now, to see how different this war would be from any before it, and especially from the wars fought by Napoleon fifty years before. Most officers considered Napoleon their perfect ideal; but things had changed.

In the Napoleonic era, the infantryman's musket was effective only to a hundred yards, and inaccurate at that range. The new rifled muskets were deadly to twice that range, and could kill at half a mile. Napoleonic artillerymen knew they were safe from the infantry's weapons; that was no longer the case.

Napoleonic armies marched where they had to go, so reinforcements could arrive no faster than men could walk. Here, Johnston's army had been brought up quickly by railroad to join Beauregard's.

Cavalry, on the other hand, was losing its effectiveness as a destructive force. Massed rifle fire made cavalry charges all but suicidal for the horseman. Cavalry's role was in intelligence — scouting enemy positions, and blocking the hostile scouts — and swift raids on lightly defended targets such as supply depots or telegraph stations.

One important lesson for the war to come *was* learned at Bull Run: in their first serious combat, the Confederacy won a clear-cut victory, driving the Yankees from the field. The Federals learned that the Rebels would not be defeated easily; that, if they really wanted to keep the United States together, they would have to fight for it.

Napoleon, who said that "in war, the moral is to the physical as three to one," would have understood that perfectly.

P.G.T. Beauregard 1818-1893
Confederate Army

Pierre Gustave Toutant Beauregard's service to the Confederacy spanned nearly the entire Civil War. It was Beauregard who gave the order to bombard Fort Sumter. Beauregard helped ensure the Confederate victory at First Bull Run, and he assumed command in the midst of battle when General Albert Sidney Johnston received a mortal wound at Shiloh. He kept Union troops bottled up at Bermuda Hundred and, although outnumbered, delayed the enemy's advance until General Lee could arrive to defend Petersburg.

But he also quarreled with Confederate President Jefferson Davis, calling him "either demented or a traitor, a living specimen of gall and hatred." Beauregard would have been wise to hold his tongue; Davis personally blocked Beauregard's military ambitions.

Born in New Orleans, Beauregard returned to Louisiana after the war. There he became president of the New Orleans, Jackson & Mississippi Railway and then Commissioner of Public Works for New Orleans.

Irvin McDowell 1818-1885
Union Army

Thrust into command and prodded by President Lincoln to attack, Irvin McDowell failed. His untested army recoiled from the Confederates at First Bull Run causing considerable apprehension in Washington, D.C. and widespread jubilation in Richmond. Despite the fact that both Union and Confederate armies were, in Lincoln's words "green alike," McDowell had the misfortune of commanding the losing novices. As a result, his first ever field command provided a dismal opening chapter in a Civil War career that never achieved distinction.

Following another ineffective performance, this time at Second Bull Run, McDowell earned a transfer to California, far away from the war. There he found greater success. He eventually became San Francisco's park commissioner and planned improvements in the Presidio, where he is buried.

Thomas "Stonewall" Jackson 1824-1863
Confederate Army

First Bull Run provided the Confederacy with its first battlefield hero. As the fighting raged, General Bee rallied his own troops by pointing toward Thomas Jackson on the hill above. "There stands Jackson like a stone wall," Bee is reported to have said. The name stuck as Jackson performed with determination that day and throughout a series of now legendary battles with Union troops in the Shenandoah Valley, at Antietam, and at Second Bull Run.

Paired with Robert E. Lee, former VMI professor Stonewall Jackson supplied the South with military genius unmatched by Union commanders in the early years of the war. The success they achieved gave the Confederacy a sense of hope. At Chancellorsville, they prepared a battle plan that historians still call an astounding triumph.

But Chancellorsville proved to be Jackson's last battle. At day's end, on a smoky and confused battlefield, Jackson's own troops mistook his reconnaissance party for the enemy and shot him. Doctors amputated Jackson's mangled left arm. Prophetically, Lee wrote to his injured comrade, "You have lost your left arm. I have lost my right." Jackson died a week later.

BIOGRAPHIES

Writer **William Messner-Loebs** was born in Michigan and raised in Huntsville, Alabama and New Orleans. In college he majored in history, concentrating on Black Studies and the Far East, with minors in Art and Philosophy. He has created comics such as WELCOME TO HEAVEN, DR. FRANKLIN; JOURNEY, a story about frontier life in Michigan in the 1810s and EPICURUS THE SAGE, his highly acclaimed satire on classical Greek philosophy published by Piranha Press. He has a long list of comic-writing credits, including WONDER WOMAN, FLASH, HAWKMAN, THE MAXX, THOR, JOHNNY QUEST and DR. FATE. He is currently writing IMPULSE for DC Comics and continues to be on the Board of Cascade Inc.—The Civil War Muster of Jackson, Michigan.

Artist/writer **Richard Waring Rockwell** has been a leading American illustrator for over four decades. Mr. Rockwell's many assignments have ranged from Creative Assistant and historic advisor for Milton Caniff's STEVE CANYON comic strip series (1953-1988) to reportage artist for clients such as NBC, CBS, CNN, CNBC, WPIX, Fox, Five, Harpers Magazine and the Herald Tribune. He has also taught at New York University, the Parsons School of Design and the Fashion Institute of Technology. He is the nephew of American artist/illustrator Norman Rockwell. He holds a B.A. and M.F.A. in art and is a decorated World War II pilot.

Fred Fredericks, inker, who studied at the School of Visual Arts in New York City is not a novice to using the comic art style for a historical venue. In the late 1950's he wrote and illustrated NEW JERSEY PATRIOTS, a daily comic strip about the Revolutionary War and then, during the Civil War centennial, he created UNDER THE STARS AND BARS, a strip about the Civil War as told from the Confederate point of view. He worked for Dell Publishing from 1960-1965 writing and illustrating such titles as THE MUNSTERS, MISTER ED, ROCKY AND BULLWINKLE, DANIEL BOONE and others. Since 1965 he has drawn MANDRAKE THE MAGICIAN for King Features, one of the most durable daily strips in circulation. A regularly featured inker at Marvel, Mr. Fredericks' recent work includes THE PUNISHER and a host of others.

Colorist **Marie Severin** began her career in comics in 1953 as staff colorist for the legendary E.C. line of horror, mystery, action-adventure and science fiction comics. After serving a brief stint with Timely comics (the predecessor of Marvel Comics), she put her skills to work in the commercial field—highlighted with a commission by the Federal Reserve Board in which she produced comics, filmstrips and sculpted figurines in a project to describe the workings of the Federal Reserve System. Ms. Severin returned to Marvel in 1964 and shortly began to take on art chores in titles such as DR. STRANGE, SUB-MARINER and HULK. Her work on KULL THE CONQUEROR, a sword-and-sorcery series, remains one of the most highly praised series that Marvel has published. She was a regular contributor to CRAZY and NOT BRAND ECHH, Marvel's humor magazines in which her abilities as cartoonist and caricaturist were showcased.

HISTORICAL COMICS™

EPIC BATTLES OF THE
CIVIL WAR

Published by:
Historical Souvenir Co.
2555 Orthodox Street
Philadelphia, PA 19137